Xmas
2005

To Bob —
The "very" "best" brother
anyone can ever hope to have

God bless you & your family
now & always !

With lots of love,
Toots / Lloyd
& family

Thanks a bunch

pictures of verse
by

Sandra Magsamen

gift

stewart tabori & chang

Like seeds
in the wind
your Kindness
travels
far

Your generosity places you firmly in the sky as a star.

You are an
inspiration
in all that
you
do . . .

your goodness
and thoughtfulness
are
true blue.

Your
exceptional
acts of kindness
have touched
many a heart...

and your
understanding
and compassion
set
you
apart

You give to others effortlessly,

and your caring actions have taught me to see...

that giving
to others
builds friendship
and
community.

Your support I will never forget...

I will forever be in your debt.

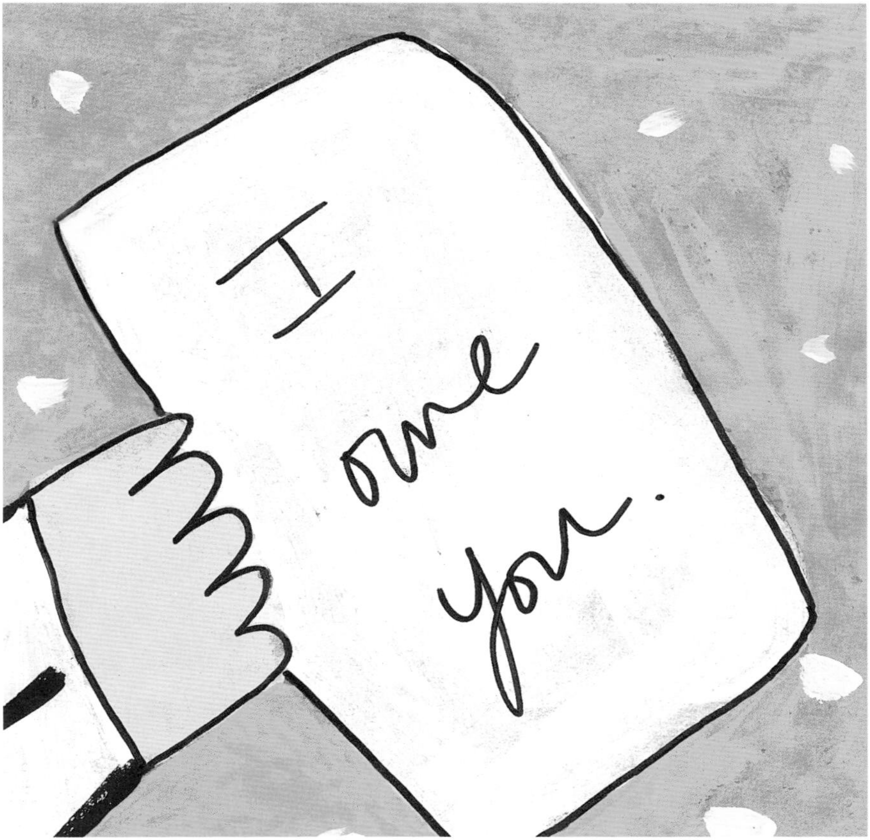
I owe you.

Thank you,
thank you,
thank you...

for all
that
you
do . . .

I sincerely express my gratitude to you,

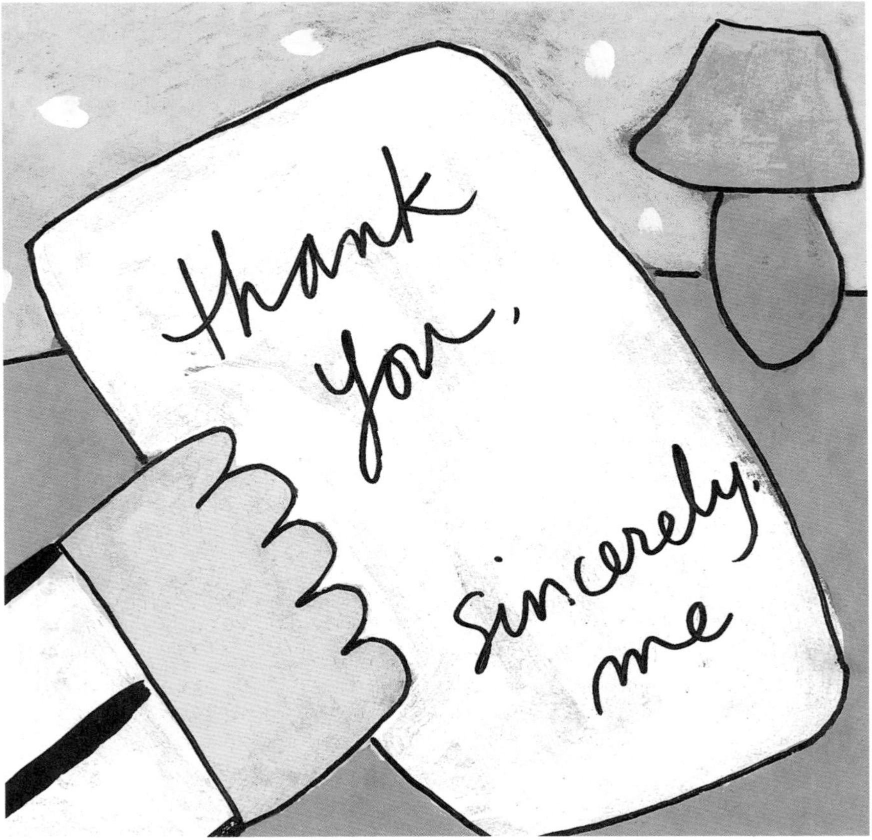
thank you,
sincerely.
me

and a
heart
felt
thank you.

Pictures and verse by Sandra Magsamen
© 2000 Hanny Girl Productions, Inc.
Exclusive licensing agent Momentum Partners, Inc., NY, NY

Published in 2000 by
Stewart, Tabori & Chang
A division of U.S. Media Holdings, Inc.
115 West 18th Street
New York, NY 10011

Distributed in Canada by
General Publishing Company Ltd.
30 Lesmill Road
Don Mills, Ontario, Canada M3B 2T6

ISBN: 1-58479-006-7

Printed in Hong Kong

10 9 8 7 6 5 4 3 2 1